High Voice

15 EASY FOLKSONG ARRANGEMENTS
FOR THE PROGRESSING SINGER
EDITED BY RICHARD WALTERS

T0048242

CONTENTS

To access companion recorded full performances
and piano accompaniments online, visit:
www.halleonard.com/mylibrary

3838-7834-2415-1372

Singers on the Recordings: * Tanya Kruse, soprano, ** Steven Stolen, tenor, *** Stuart Mitchell, tenor
Pianists on the Recordings: Catherine Bringerud, Christopher Ruck, and Richard Walters

ISBN 978-0-634-07727-2

HAL•LEONARD®
CORPORATION
7777 W. BLUEMOUND RD. P.O.BOX 13819 MILWAUKEE, WI 53213

In Australia Contact:
Hal Leonard Australia Pty. Ltd.
4 Lentara Court
Cheltenham, Victoria, 3192 Australia
Email: ausadmin@halleonard.com.au

Visit Hal Leonard Online at
www.halleonard.com

NOTES ON THE SONGS

The Ash Grove

This Welsh tune, known as "Llwyn On," must date before the early 18th century, as it appeared in altered form in John Gay's *The Beggar's Opera* (1728). It was first published, without words, in 1802. Some lyrics appeared by 1809. The song text has been attributed to John Oxenford, although there are several different sets of verses, including parodies added after the melody was published. "The Ash Grove" is clearly a nostalgic place associated with friends of childhood, perhaps even being a cemetery.

Barbara Allen

The song, first mentioned in Samuel Pepys' Diaries in 1666, originated somewhere in the British Isles; both English and Scottish origins have been cited. Some speculation has been that William in the song is a knight. We can only guess why Barbara Allen broke William's heart. There have been countless versions of the song found in England, Scotland, Ireland, US and Canada, a natural mutation that is common to old folksongs.

Drink to Me Only with Thine Eyes

The words are from the poem "To Celia" by the great English poet and playwright Ben Jonson (1572-1637). The origin of the tune is unknown, but it dates from the late 18th century, after 1770. This melody has been attributed to Mozart, but that is unlikely and has not been substantiated. This is a tender, heartfelt, intimate expression of love. A performer should sing smoothly and sincerely. An alternative version of this song has a lyric by Jane Taylor (1783-1824), with music ascribed to Dr. H. Harrington (1727-1816).

Greensleeves

This English song, popular for centuries, was first mentioned in the "Stationers' Register" in 1580, which licensed Richard Jones to print "A new Northern Dittye of the Lady Greensleeves." Legend has it that Henry VIII wrote this while courting Ann Boleyn, but that is almost surely false. This same melody was later set to different words by American William Chatterton Dix in the the 19th century, called "What Child Is This." Lady Greensleeves is probably a secret, illicit mistress.

How Can I Keep from Singing

This American tune is possibly by Robert Lowry, published in 1869 in his "Bright Jewels for the Sunday School," although the melody is more likely of folk origin. The text has been sometimes attributed to 19th century writer Anna Warner (author of the first verse of "Jesus Loves Me"), although this credit is not conclusive. This sturdy tune is sometimes still used as a hymn. "Singing" in the context of the song could be a joyful expression of faith, or it could be a metaphor for speaking out in the face of injustice. Such was the context of folk singer/activist Pete Seeger's recording of the song.

I Gave My Love a Cherry

This mountain song from Kentucky (probably from the early 19th century) is also known as "The Riddle Song." In the final verse, where the riddle is solved, the line "a chicken when it's pippin' " refers to the undeveloped bird in the egg ("pippin' " is a dialect rendition of "peeping"). This is a tender love song that should be performed with graceful, earnest emotion.

I Know Where I'm Goin'

This ballad is probably of Scottish origin, although it might be English. A possible interpretation would be of a young woman living at home. Her parents have forbidden her to see Johnny. She longs for the nice things she knows that poor Johnny cannot provide her, but is consumed by love for him. Against her parents' wishes, she knows she's going to secretly steal away to be with Johnny. This song has been recorded by various artists, including Judy Collins on her first album in 1961.

Johnny Has Gone for a Soldier

The music for this American Revolutionary War song was adapted from the 17th century Irish song "Sìul a Ruin," translated from Gaelic as "A blessing walk with you, my love." The song is also known as "I Wish I Were on Yonder Hill," "Buttermilk Hill," "Shule Agra" and "Sweet William;" the lyrics for each of these vary greatly. According to one theory, the tune "Shule Agra" arose out of the Glorious Revolution in Ireland in 1688. Beyond heartbreak and worry, the young woman in "Johnny Has Gone for a Soldier" has been left alone by a sweetheart or husband gone off to war, leaving her few options for employment in 18th century America. Her line "I'll dye my dress, I'll dye it red" hints that she is desperate enough, at least momentarily, to consider harlotry as an avenue of survival.

Loch Lomond

Loch Lomond is the largest lake in Scotland, located in the west of the country. This tune is of Scottish origin, an old Jacobite air based on an older folk tune "Robin Cushie" ("Kind Robin Loves Me") found in McGibbons' Scots Tunes Book I (1742). The words are attributed to Lady John Scott (1810-1900). The version we are familiar with today probably first appeared in print in Poets and Poetry of Scotland (1876). The chorus refers to two Jacobite soldiers captured by the British—one who was to be hanged, and the other who was to be set free to return to Scotland to warn all Scots what would happen if they fought for their freedom again. The Jacobite to be hanged said to the other "you take the high road, and I'll take the low road and I'll be in Scotland afore ye," meaning the high road is the road of the living, and the low road is for those whom have passed into the spirit world through death. He believed that in this way he would be with his wife before the free man. Ben Lomond is the large hill situated next to Loch Lomond. "Greetin' " is Scottish for grieving in the line, " The woeful may cease from their greetin'."

Scarborough Fair

This folksong is from England, dating from the 16th or 17th centuries. It may have been adapted from an older ballad, "The Elfin Bride." Scarborough Fair was a huge 45 day trading event starting every August 15 which drew people from all over England and Europe. There have been many different variants of the words and melody. Herbs were significant to medieval people. Parsley was thought to soothe bitterness; sage was thought to give strength; rosemary was a symbol of faithfulness; thyme represented courage. The key to understanding the cryptic meaning lies in verse five: "Love imposes impossible tasks... though not more than any heart asks." Simon & Garfunkel recorded a famous version of the song (with a slightly different melody) for their album *Parsley, Sage, Rosemary and Thyme*, which became a popular hit in1968.

Shenandoah

This famous folksong, a very symbol of Americana, may have originated as a chanty (a song sung by sailors), possibly sung by early American river men or Canadian voyageurs. Its date is unknown, but it is possibly from the late 18th or early 19th centuries. Two verses first appeared in print in an article by W.J. Alden in *Harpers* magazine in 1882. There are many different interpretations of the mysterious lyrics. Shenandoah was an Indian chief who lived on the Missouri River. Shenandoah is also the name of a river and region in Virginia. Whatever its specific meaning, the song is certainly about homesickness for people and places left behind.

Soldier, Soldier, Will You Marry Me

This American folksong of the 18th century is probably an adaptation of an English tune. This is a flirtatious, comic character song. A performer needs to understand clearly which character is singing: the maiden, the soldier, or the narrator. Make a distinct difference for each of the voices in your singing. Rudyard Kipling (1865-1936) wrote a poem "Soldier, Soldier," along the same sentiments, which was set to music in 1898 by Percy Grainger. Except for subject matter, it is unrelated to the old folksong.

The Streets of Laredo

This song, also known as the "Cowboy's Lament," is based on the Irish songs "A Handful of Laurel" and "The Bard of Armagh." Other American songs borrowed the same tune. The lyrics for "The Streets of Laredo" were first published in *The American Songbag* in 1927, edited by poet Carl Sandburg. The song has been recorded by many artists in various styles. The dying young cowboy, who probably led a rough, rowdy and lonely life, becomes sentimental as his death quickly approaches, revealing a surprisingly poetic character. A singer should be sensitive to telling the story of the song.

The Water Is Wide

This song originated in the British Isles (either of English or Irish origin). It was first published in 1724 with the title "O Waly, Waly." The most familiar version of this folksong was collected in Somerset by Cecil Sharp. The song shares some verses with a longer ballad, "Lord Jamie Douglas," although it is possible that "O Waly, Waly" existed first. "The Water Is Wide" and "O Waly, Waly" share a similar melody, and have some verse overlap. "The Water Is Wide" version became more common in the 19th century. The song is about the broken heart of someone who was deceived by a false-hearted lover, who apparently left without warning and sailed away. The most famous setting of the tune was by English composer Benjamin Britten (1913-1976).

When Johnny Comes Marching Home

This American song of the Civil War was credited to Union Army bandmaster Patrick S. Gilmore (1863), written under the pseudonym Louis Lambert. The words were written to the tune "To the Army and Navy of the Union" (composer unknown). The song was sung by both the North and South as they awaited the return home of their soldiers during wartime. It is similar to the Irish song "Johnny I Hardly Knew Ye," about a maimed soldier, though it is not known which song came first. The singer of the song could be any person who cares about Johnny. (Johnny was a common name in the 18th and 19th century, essentially meaning every man.) For women singers, it may help to consider Johnny as a departed husband or lover, which adds urgency to the performance.

The Ash Grove

Welsh Folksong ("Llwyn On")
arranged by Bryan Stanley

Allegretto

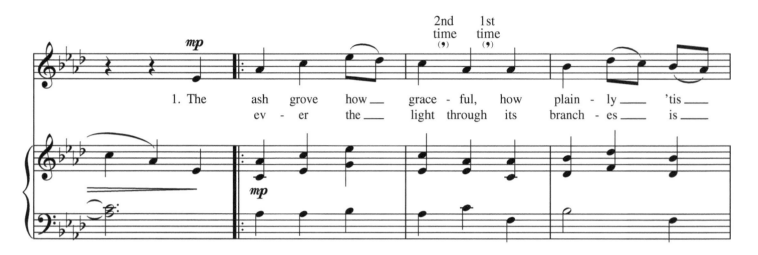

1. The ash grove how __ grace - ful, how plain - ly __ 'tis __
ev - er the __ light through its branch - es __ is __

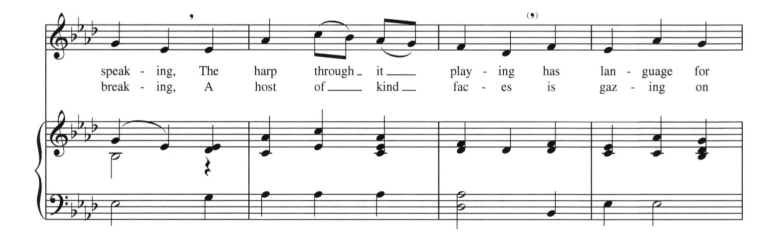

speak - ing, The harp through _ it __ play - ing has lan - guage for
break - ing, A host of __ kind __ fac - es is gaz - ing on

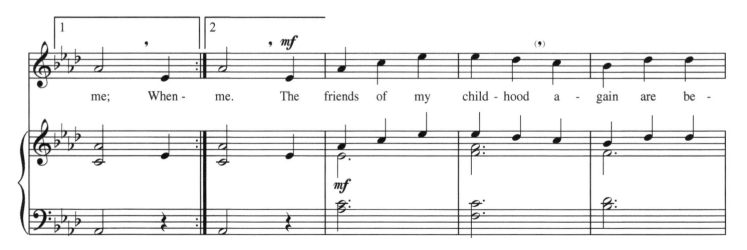

me; When me. The friends of my child - hood a - gain are be -

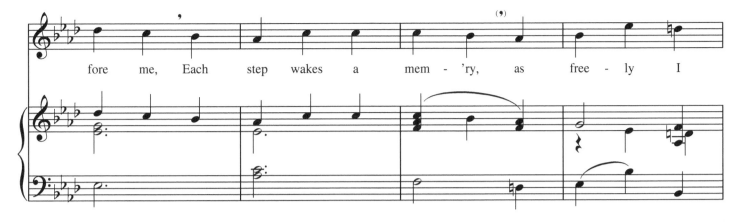

fore me, Each step wakes a mem - 'ry, as free - ly I

poco rit. *a tempo*

roam, With soft whis - pers ___ lad - en, its leaves rus - tle ___

poco rit. *a tempo*

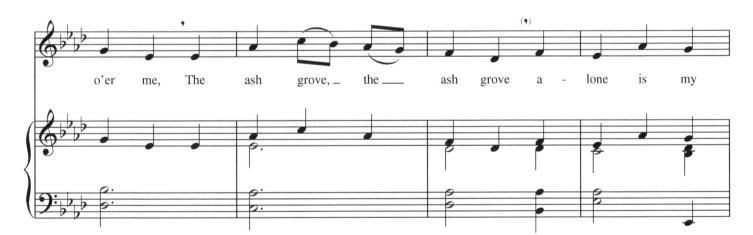

o'er me, The ash grove, _ the ___ ash grove a - lone is my

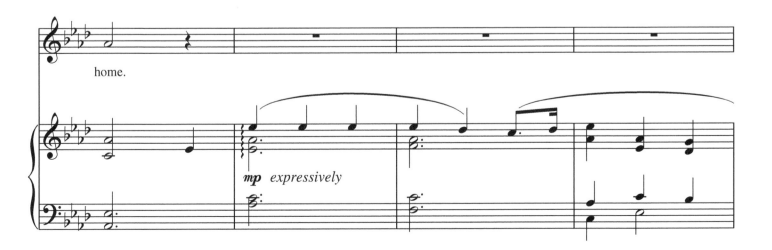

home.

mp expressively

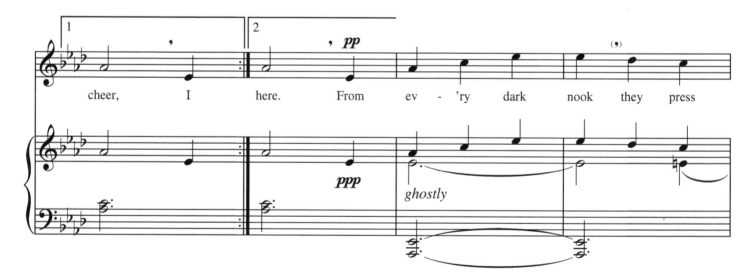

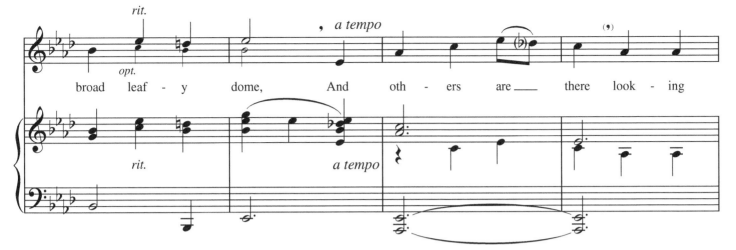

broad leaf-y dome, And oth-ers are ___ there look-ing

down-ward __ to __ greet me, The ash grove, __ the __ ash grove a-

lone is my home. The ash grove, __ the __

ash grove _____ a - lone is my home.

Barbara Allen

Scottish Folksong
arranged by Bryan Stanley

Moderato ♩ = 88

mf melancholy

1. In Scar - let Town, where I was born; There was a fair maid dwell - in', Made ev - 'ry youth cry___ Well - a - day! Her name was Bar - b'ra Al - len. 'Twas in the mer - ry month of May, When

2. He sent a ser - vant to the town, The place where she was dwell - in'. "My mas - ter's sick and___ bids you come If you be Bar - b'ra Al - len." And as she crossed the wood - ed fields, She

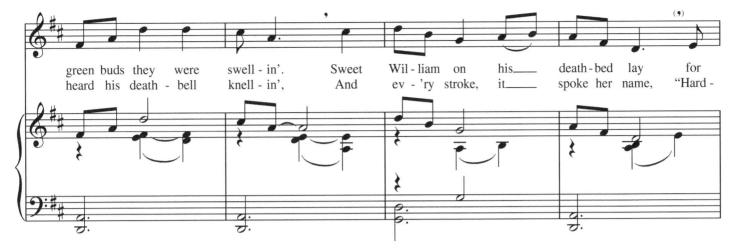

green buds they were swell - in'. Sweet Wil - liam on his___ death - bed lay for
heard his death - bell knell - in', And ev - 'ry stroke, it___ spoke her name, "Hard -

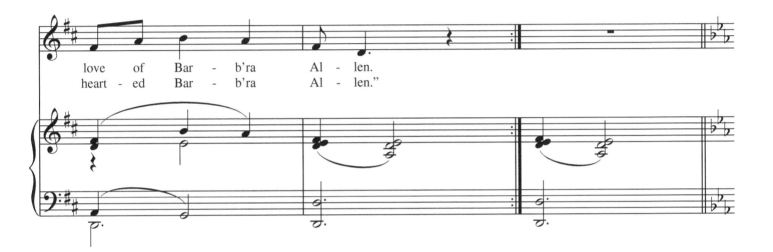

love of Bar - b'ra Al - len.
heart - ed Bar - b'ra Al - len."

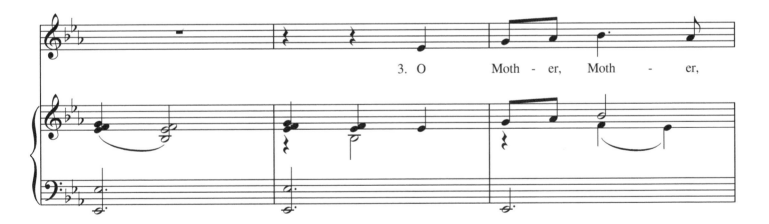

3. O Moth - er, Moth - er,

make my bed, And make it long and nar - row. Sweet

10

William died for love of me; I'll die for him of sor - row." "Fare -

well," she said, "ye maid - ens all, And shun the fault I fell in: Hence -

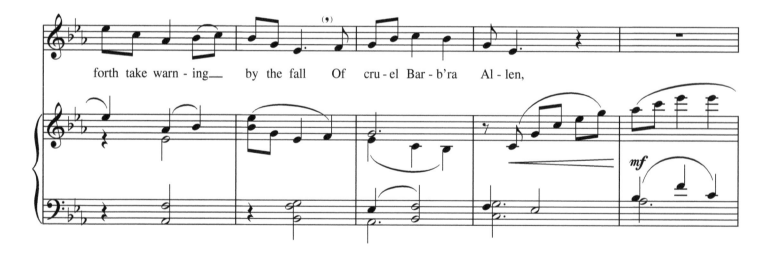

forth take warn - ing__ by the fall Of cru - el Bar - b'ra Al - len,

cru - el Bar - b'ra Al - len."__

Drink to Me Only with Thine Eyes

Poem ("To Celia")
Ben Jonson (1572-1637)

Music based on an English Folksong
arranged by Brian Dean

I'll___ not look for wine. The

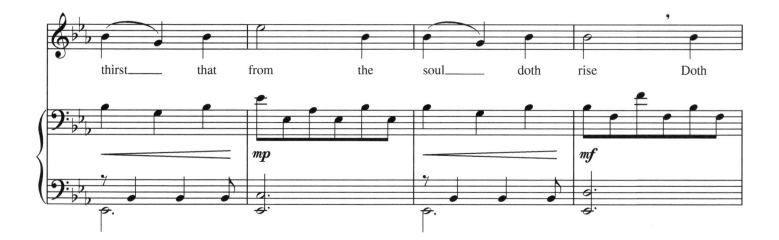

thirst___ that from the soul___ doth rise Doth

ask a drink___ di - vine;___

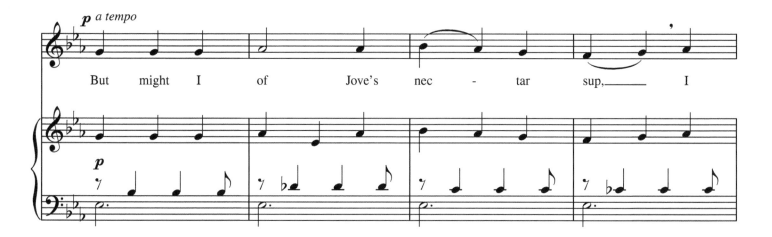

But might I of Jove's nec - tar sup,___ I

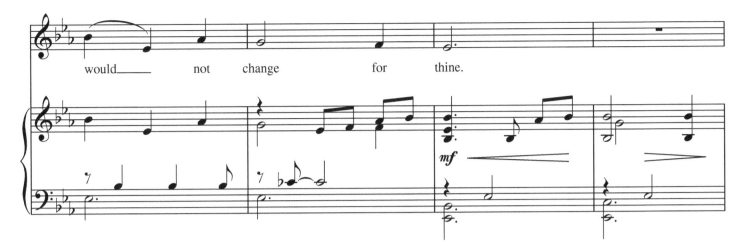

would____ not change for thine.

2. I sent thee late a

ro - sy wreath,____ Not so____ much hon - 'ring

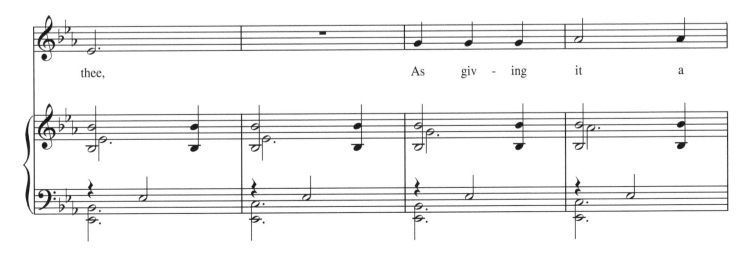

thee, As giv - ing it a

14

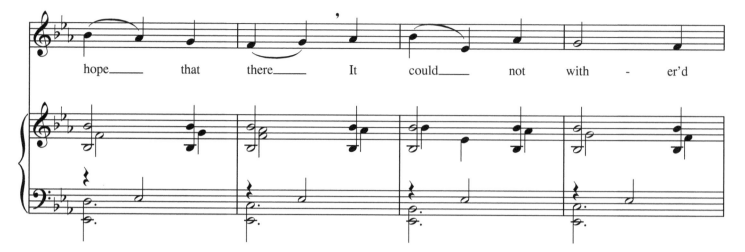

hope____ that there____ It could____ not with - er'd

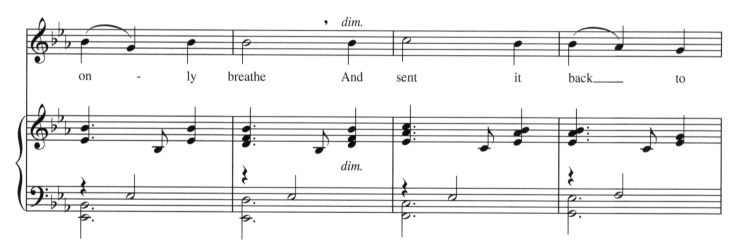

be; But thou____ there - on didst

on - ly breathe And sent it back____ to

me,_____

A little slower

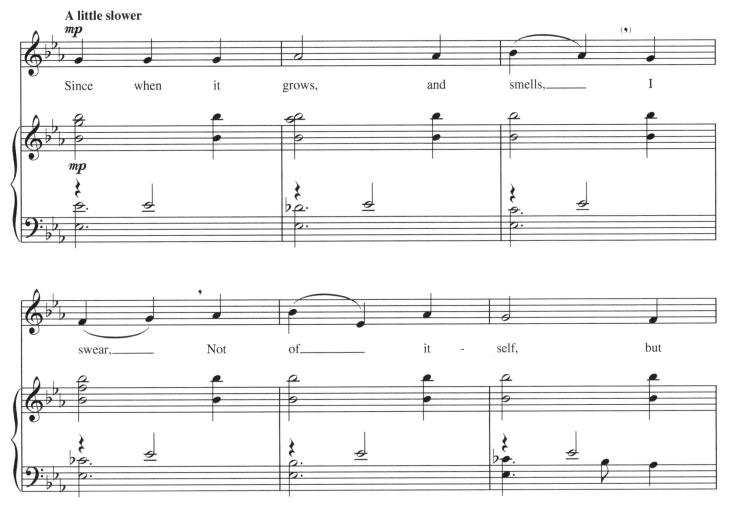

Since when it grows, and smells,_____ I

swear,_____ Not of_____ it - self, but

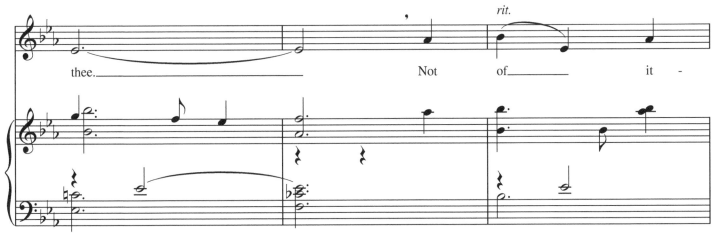

thee._____ Not of_____ it -

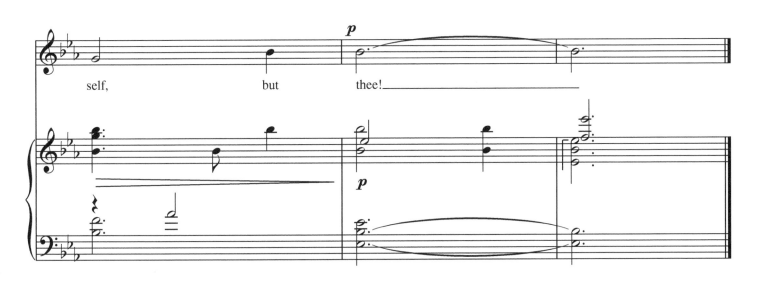

self, but thee!_____

Greensleeves

16th Century English Folksong
arranged by Bryan Stanley

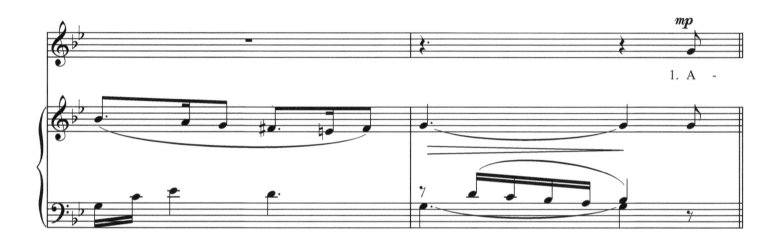

las, my love,_____ you do me wrong to
vows you've bro - ken, like my heart, Oh,

cast me off_____ dis - cour - teous - ly, Though I have loved you so
why did you so en - rap - ture me? Now I re - main in a

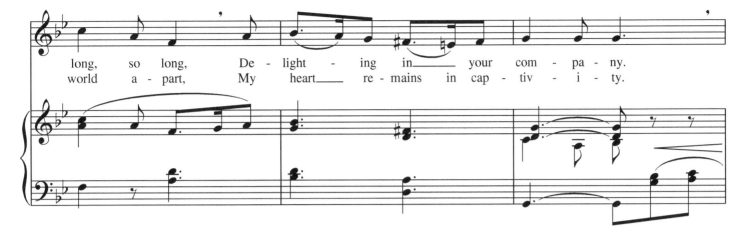

long, so long, De - light - ing in___ your com - pa - ny.
world a - part, My heart___ re - mains in cap - tiv - i - ty.

Green - sleeves___ was all my joy, Green - sleeves___ was

my de - light. Green - sleeves was my heart of gold, Oh

who___ but La - dy Green - sleeves? 2. Your

Green - sleeves?

3. I

with pedal

have been read - y at your hand to

grant what - ev - er you would crave. I have both wa - gered

life and land, Your love and good will for to have.

Green - sleeves___ was all my joy, Green - sleeves___ was

my de - light. Green - sleeves was my

heart of gold, Oh who_____ but La - dy

Green - sleeves? Who_____ but La - dy Green - sleeves?

How Can I Keep from Singing

Words possibly by Anna Warner

American Tune
Music possibly by Robert Lawry, 1869
arranged by Christopher Ruck

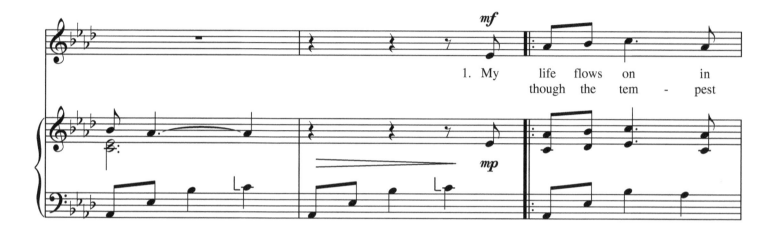

1. My life flows on in
though the tem - pest

end - less song a - bove earth's lam - en - ta - tion. I
'round me rears, I know the truth, it liv - eth. What

hear the real, though far off hymn that hails a new cre - it
though the dark - ness 'round me close, Songs in the nights it

3. When ty - rants trem - ble, sick with fear And hear their death knells ring - ing; When friends re - joice both far and near, How can I keep from sing - ing? In pris - on cell and dun - geon vile Our thoughts to them are wing - ing. When friends by shame are__

un - de - filed, How can I keep from sing - ing? No storm can shake my

poco rit.

mp

in - most calm while to that rock I'm cling - ing._____ It

poco rit.

Slower

sounds an ech - o_____ in my soul. How

p

pp

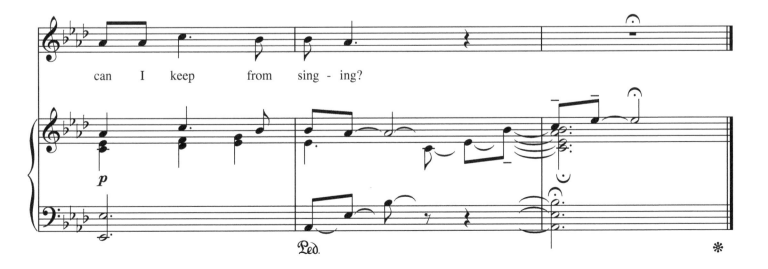

can I keep from sing - ing?

p

Ped.

I Gave My Love a Cherry

Mountain Song from Kentucky
arranged by Brian Dean

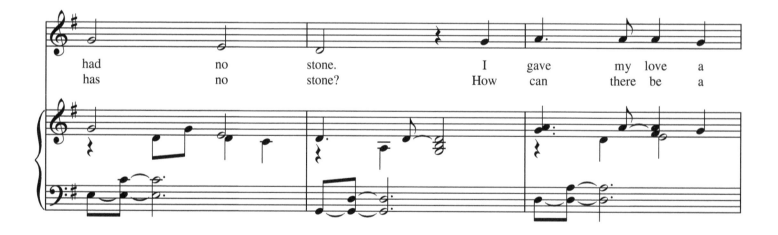

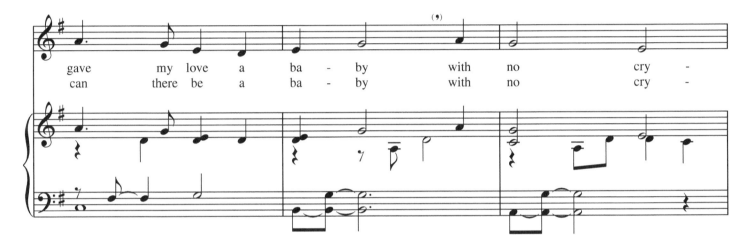

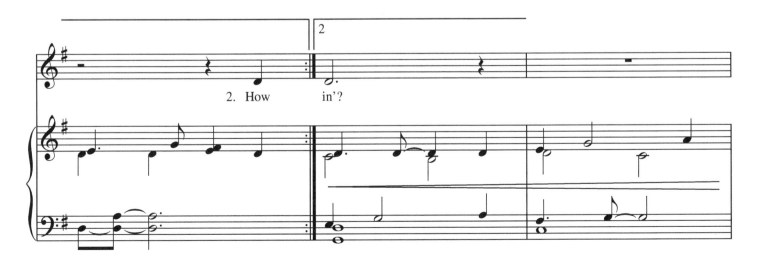

love you, it has no end._____

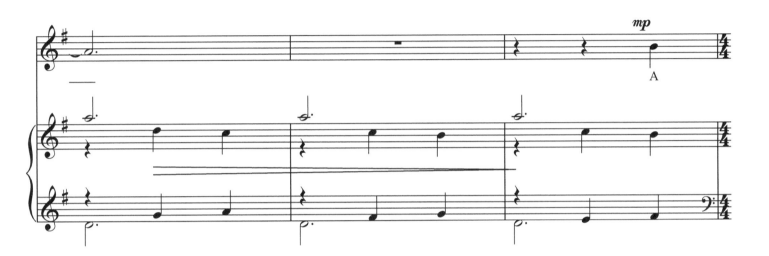

A

ba - by when it's sleep - in' makes no

cry - in'.

I Know Where I'm Goin'

Scottish Folksong
arranged by Richard Walters

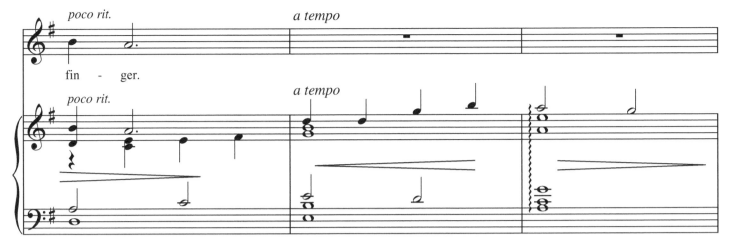

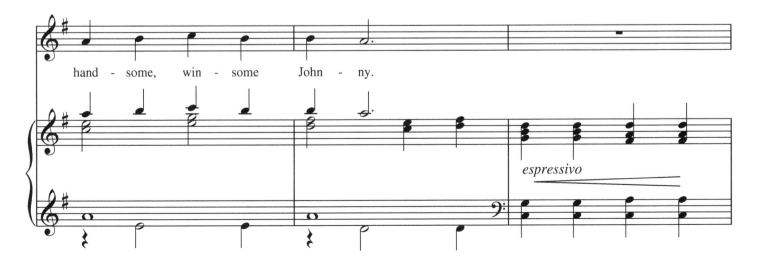

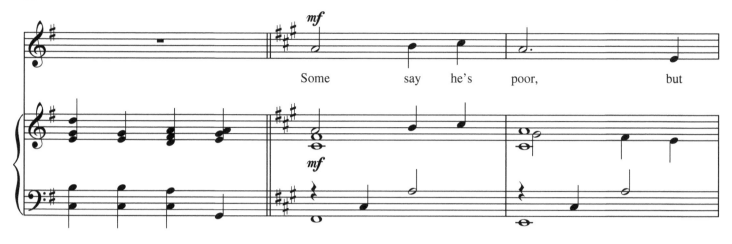

Some say he's poor, but

I say he's bon - nie. Fair - est of them all ___ is my

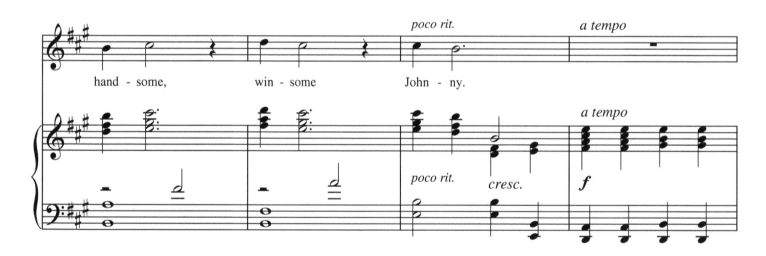

hand - some, win - some John - ny.

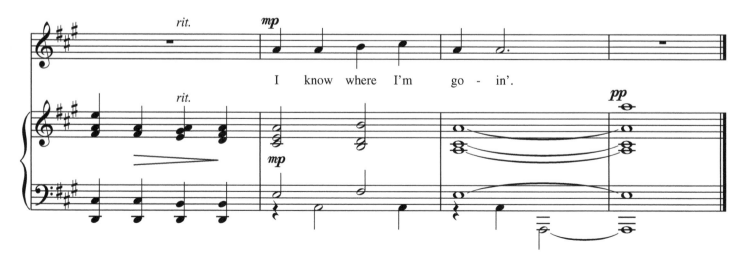

I know where I'm go - in'.

Johnny Has Gone for a Soldier

American Revolutionary War Song
Based on a 17th Century Irish tune
arranged by Richard Walters

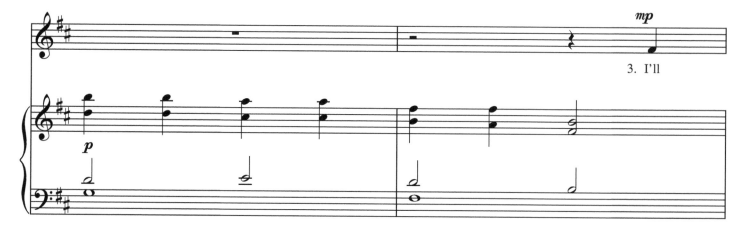

3. I'll

sell my rod, I'll sell my reel. Like - wise I'll sell my

spin - nin' wheel, and buy my love ___ a sword of steel.

John - ny has gone for a sol - dier!

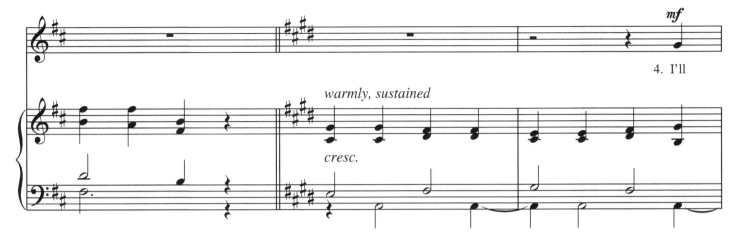

4. I'll

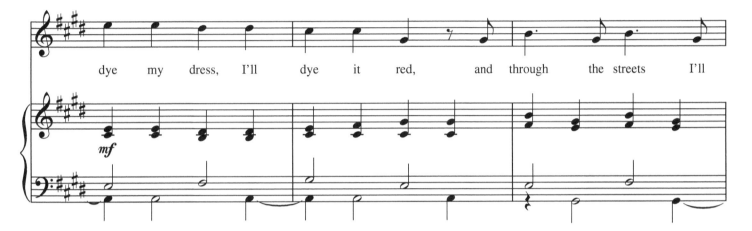

dye my dress, I'll dye it red, and through the streets I'll

beg for bread. The lad I love ___ from me has fled. ___

___ John-ny has gone for a sol - dier!

Loch Lomond

Scottish Folksong
arranged by Brian Dean

Serenely ♩ = 80-90

Lyrics:

1. By yon bon-nie banks an' yon bon-nie braes, Where the sun shines bright on Loch Lo-mond, Where me an' my true love were ev-er want to gae, On the bon-nie, bon-nie banks o' Loch Lo-mond. Oh, ye'll take the high road, an'

I'll take the low road, an' I'll be in Scot - land a - fore ye, But

me an' my true love will nev - er meet a - gain On the bon - nie, bon - nie banks o' Loch

Lo - mond. 2. 'Twas

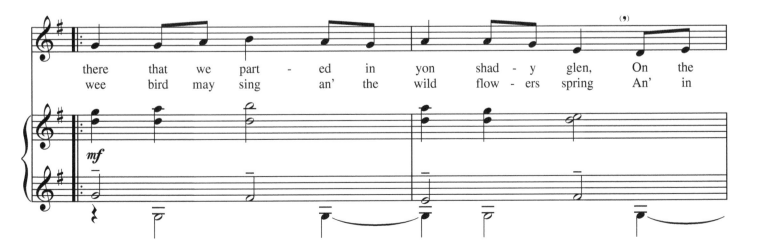

there that we part - ed in yon shad - y glen, On the
wee bird may sing an' the wild flow - ers spring An' in

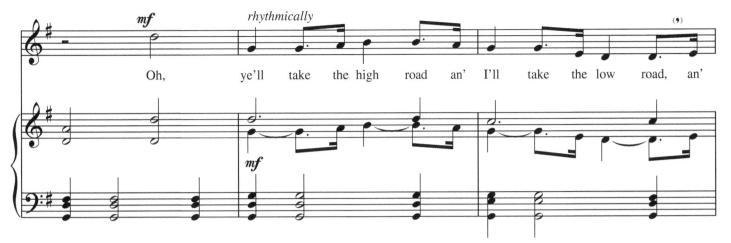

Oh, ye'll take the high road an' I'll take the low road, an'

I'll be in Scot - land a - fore ye, But me an' my true love will

nev - er meet a - gain____ On the bon - nie, bon - nie banks o' Loch

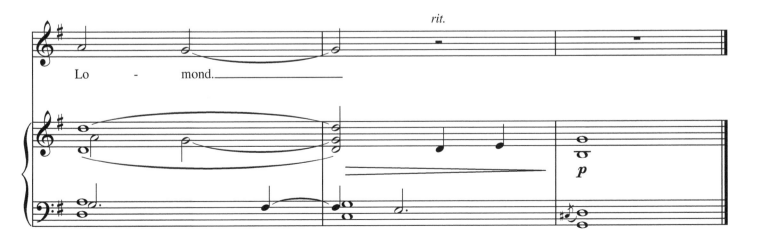

Lo - mond.____

Shenandoah

19th Century American Chanty
arranged by Richard Walters

Moderately slow

1. Oh, Shen - an - do' _____ I long to
Shen - an - do' _____ I love your

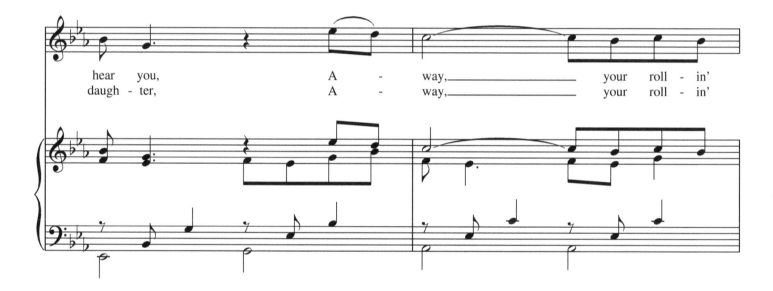

hear you, A - way, _____ your roll - in'
daugh - ter, A - way, _____ your roll - in'

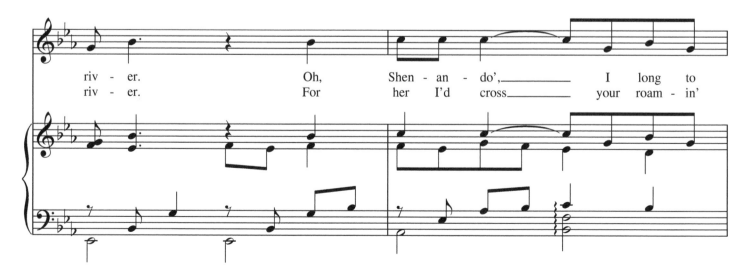

riv - er. Oh, Shen - an - do', _____ I long to
riv - er. For her I'd cross _____ your roam - in'

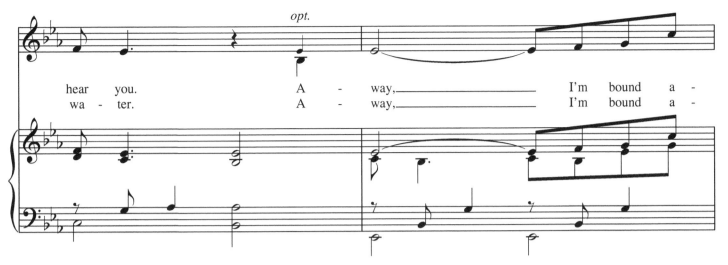

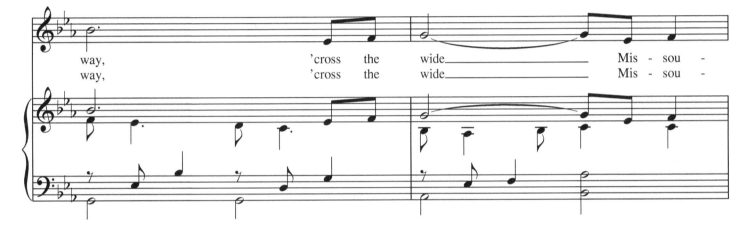

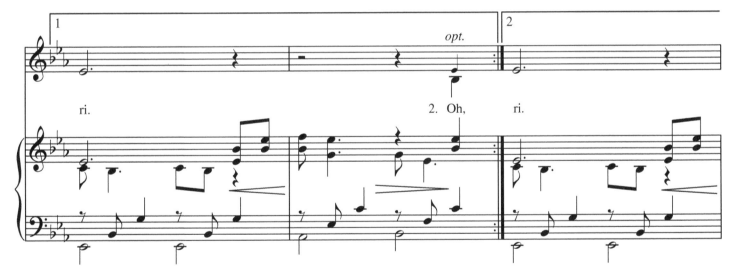

leave you, A - way____ your roll - in' riv - er. Oh,

Shen - an - do',____ I'll not de - ceive you. A - way,____ I'm bound a -

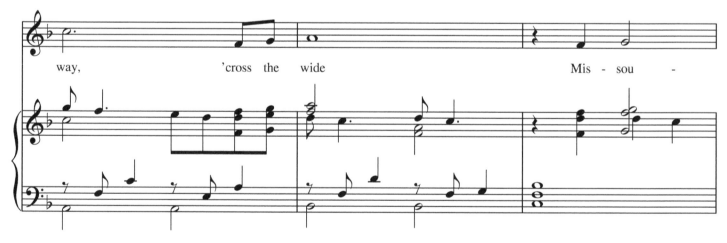

way, 'cross the wide Mis - sou -

ri.

Scarborough Fair

English Folksong
arranged by Christopher Ruck

Allegretto

1. Are you go - in' to
2. Have {him / her} make me a

Scar - bor - ough Fair?   Pars - ley sage,   rose -
cam - bric shirt,   Pars - ley sage,   rose -

mar - y and thyme._____   Re - mem - ber
mar - y and thyme,_____   With - out a

me to one who lives there,_____ For
seam or fine nee-dle work,_____ And

once { he / she } was a true love of mine.
then { he'll / she'll } be a true love of

mine.

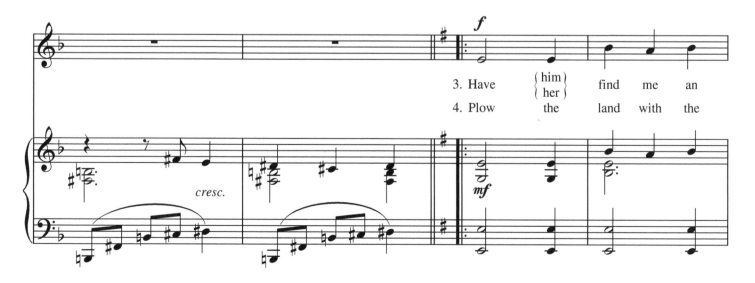

3. Have { him / her } find me an
4. Plow the land with the

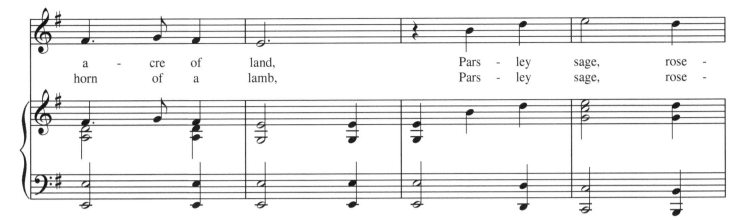

a - cre of land, Pars - ley sage, rose -
horn of a lamb, Pars - ley sage, rose -

mar - y and thyme,_____ Be - tween the
mar - y and thyme,_____ Then sow some

sea and o - ver the sand,_____ And
seeds from north of the dam,_____ And

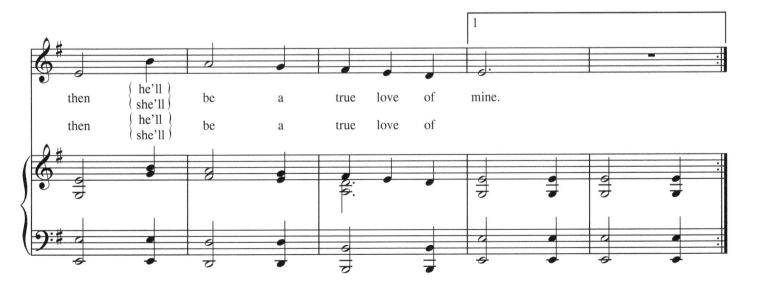

then {he'll / she'll} be a true love of mine.
then {he'll / she'll} be a true love of

mine.

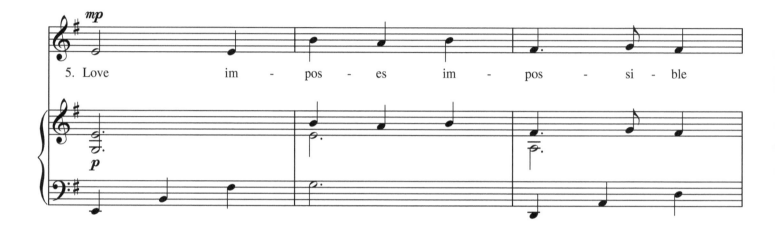

5. Love im - pos - es im - pos - si - ble

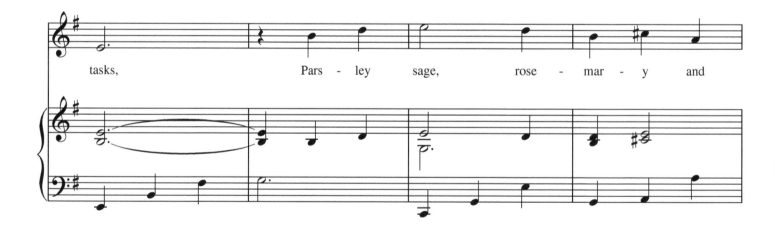

tasks, Pars - ley sage, rose - mar - y and

thyme._____ Though not_____ more than

an - y heart asks,_____ And I must

poco rit.

know $\left\{\begin{array}{l}\text{he's}\\\text{she's}\end{array}\right\}$ a true love of mine.

poco rit.

Ped. ✳

p *freely*

I must know $\left\{\begin{array}{l}\text{he's}\\\text{she's}\end{array}\right\}$ a true love of mine._____

colla voce *a tempo*

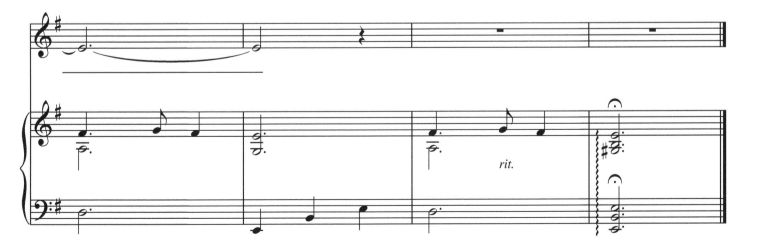

rit.

The Streets of Laredo
(Cowboy's Lament)

19th Century American Folksong
based on the Irish Ballad
"A Handful of Laurel"
arranged by Richard Walters

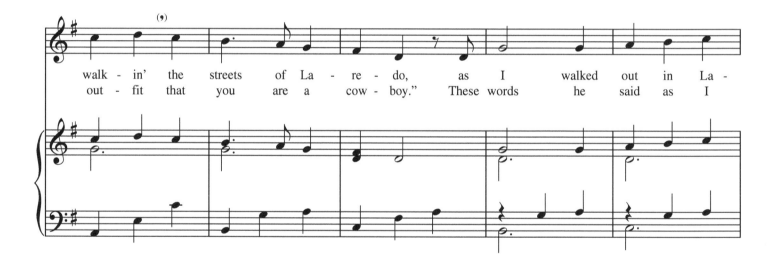

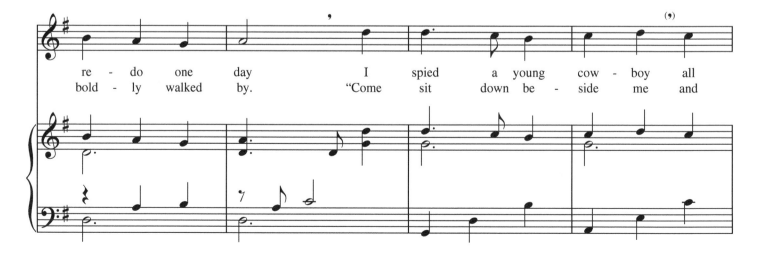

wrapped in white lin - en, all wrapped in white lin - en and
hear my sad sto - ry, I'm shot in the chest and I

1

cold as the clay. _____ 2. "I
know I must

2

die." _____ 3. "It was

1st time *mf*
2nd time *p*

(9)

once in the sad - dle I used to go dash - in',
six - teen gam - blers to car - ry my cof - fin,

1st time *mf*
2nd time *p*

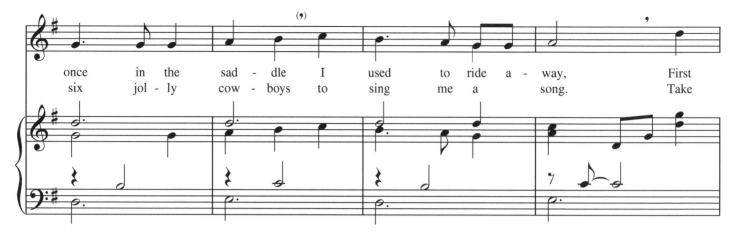

once in the sad - dle I used to ride a - way, First
six jol - ly cow - boys to used sing me a song. Take

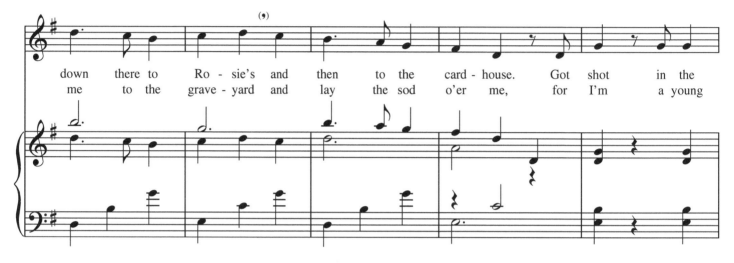

down there to Ro - sie's and then to the card - house. Got shot in the
me to the grave - yard and then lay the sod o'er me, for I'm a young

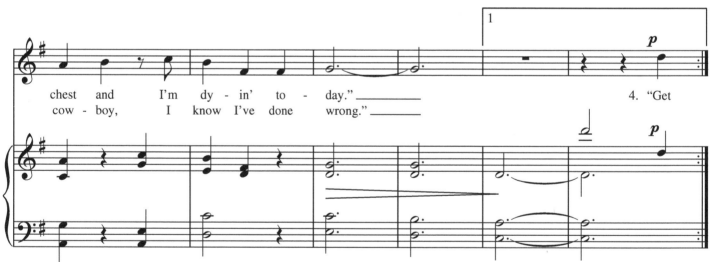

1

chest and I'm dy - in' to - day." 4. "Get
cow - boy, I know I've done wrong."

2

Slower

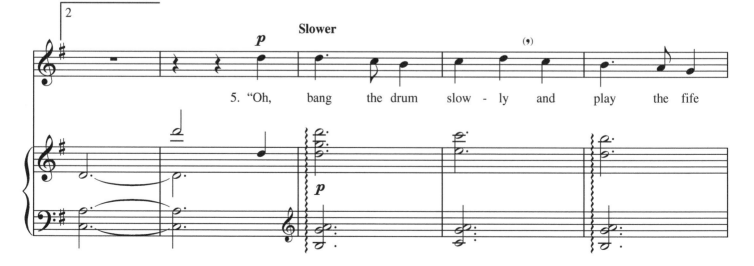

5. "Oh, bang the drum slow - ly and play the fife

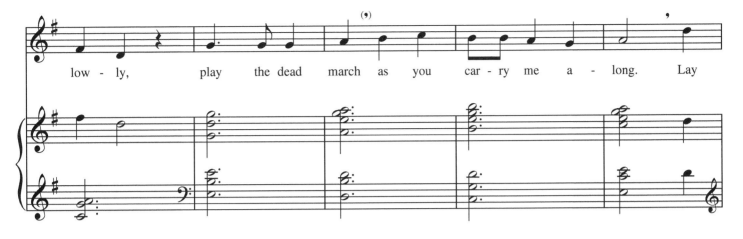

low - ly, play the dead march as you car - ry me a - long. Lay

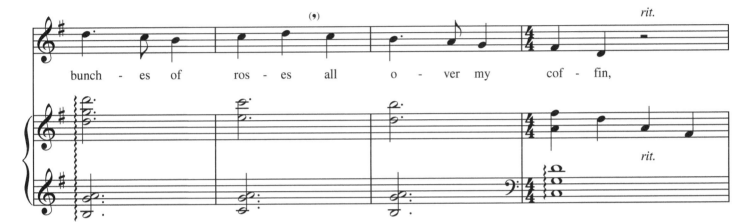

bunch - es of ros - es all o - ver my cof - fin,

More slowly

ros - es to dead - en the clods as they fall."

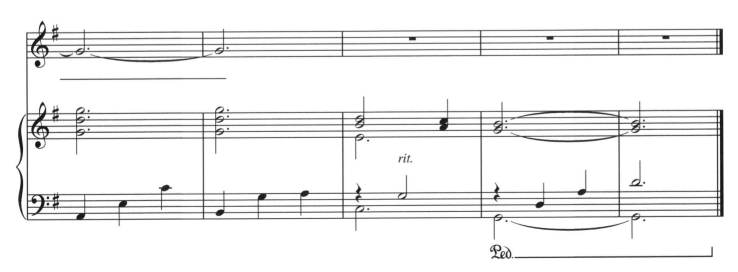

The Water Is Wide

Based on "O Waly, Waly"
English Folksong
arranged by Christopher Ruck

Moderately ♩ = ca. 72

1. The wa-ter is wide I can-not get o'er, And nei-ther
   mead - ows the oth - er day, A - gath-'ring

have I wings to __ fly. Give me a boat that will car-ry __
flow'rs a - long the __ way, A - gath-'ring flow'rs both red and __

two, And both shall row, my love and __ I.
blue, I lit-tle thought what love can __

2. O, down in the do.

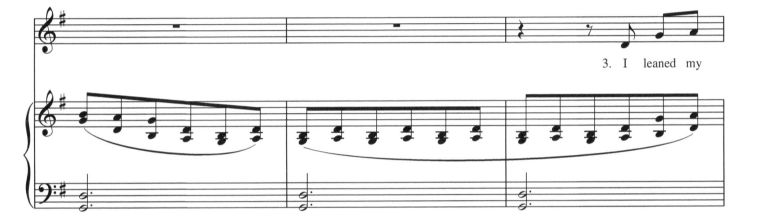

3. I leaned my

back up a-gainst some oak Think - ing that { he / she } was a trust - y ___

tree; But first { he / she } bend - ed and then { he ___ / she ___ } broke; And so did

poco rit.

my false love to __ me.

Expansively

4. A ship there is, and she sails the

sea, She's load-ed deep as deep can __ be, But not so

deep as the love I'm __ in: I know not if I sink or __

When Johnny Comes Marching Home

credited to Louis Lambert, 1863
Melody adapted from an Irish Folksong
arranged by Richard Walters

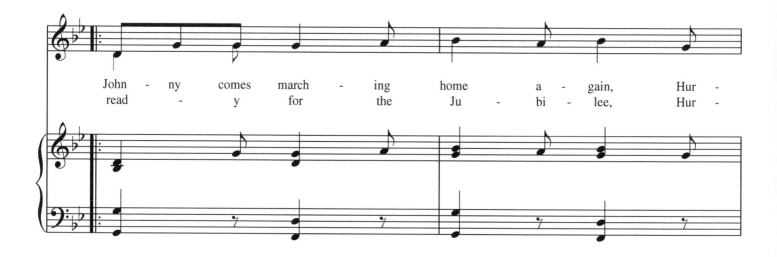

John - ny comes march - ing home a - gain, Hur -
read - y for the Ju - bi - lee, Hur -

rah! _____ Hur - rah! We'll give him a heart - y
rah! _____ Hur - rah! We'll give the he - ro

welcome then, Hur - rah! _____ Hur - rah! The
three times three, Hur - rah! _____ Hur - rah! The

cresc. *mf*

men will cheer and the boys will shout, the la - dies, they __ will
lau - rel wreath __ is read - y now to place up - on __ his

all turn out. We'll shout "hur - ray" when
loy - al brow. We'll shout "hur - ray" when

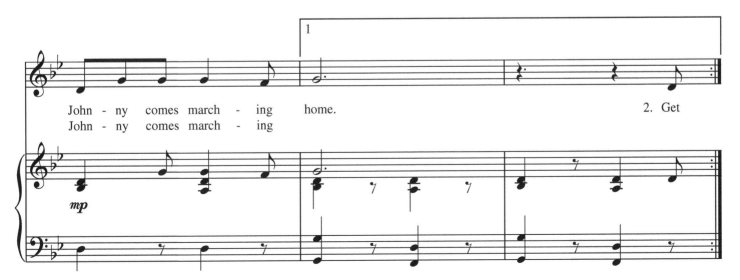

John - ny comes march - ing home.
John - ny comes march - ing

2. Get

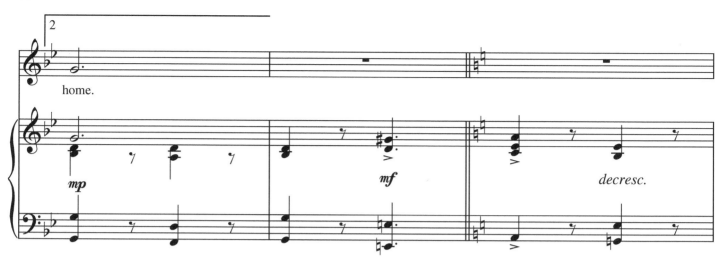

home.

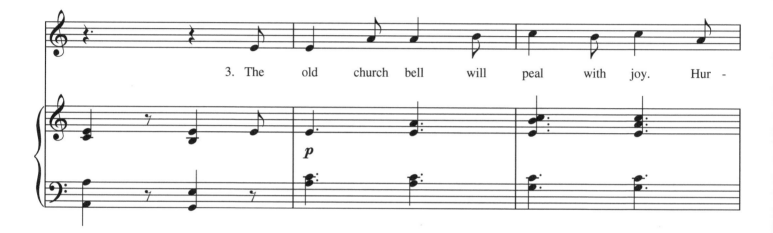

3. The old church bell will peal with joy. Hur -

rah! _____ Hur - rah! To wel - come home our

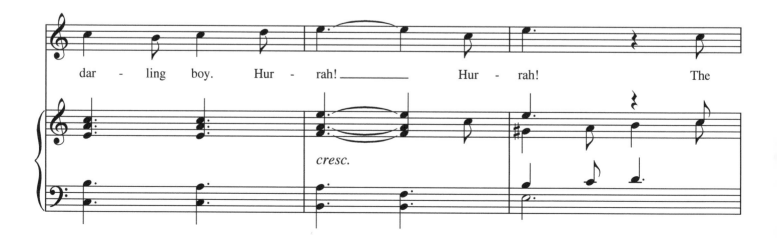

dar - ling boy. Hur - rah! _____ Hur - rah! The

vil - lage lads ___ and las - sies say with ros - es they ___ will

strew the way. We'll shout "hur - ray" when

John - ny comes march - ing home.

4. Let

love and friend - ship on that day, Hur -

rah! _____ Hur - rah! Their choic - est treas - ures

then dis - play. Hur - rah! _____ Hur - rah! And

let each one ___ per - form some part to fill with joy ___ the

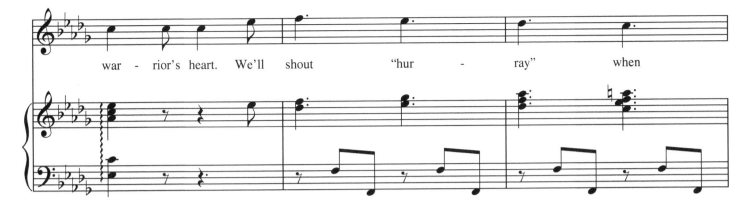

war - rior's heart. We'll shout "hur - ray" when

John - ny comes march - ing home, when John - ny comes march - ing

home, when John - ny comes march - ing, march - ing, march - ing

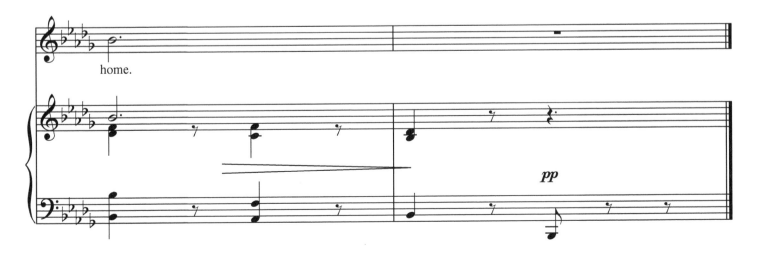

home.

Soldier, Soldier Will You Marry Me?

American Folksong
arranged by Brian Dean

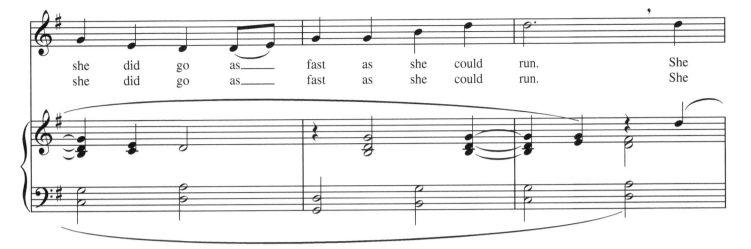

she did go as____ fast as she could run. She
she did go as____ fast as she could run. She

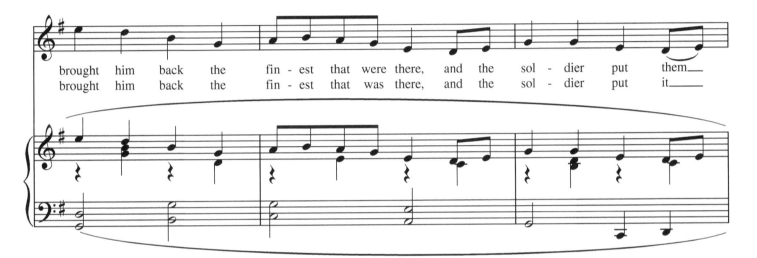

brought him back the fin - est that were there, and the sol - dier put them____
brought him back the fin - est that was there, and the sol - dier put it____

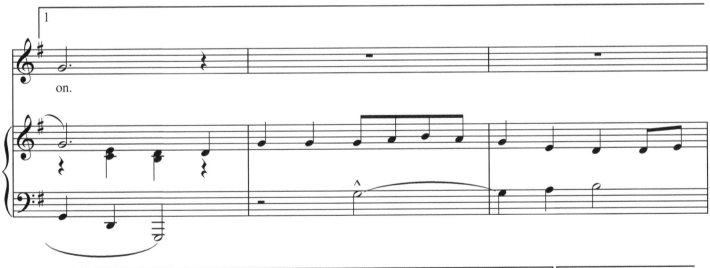

1

on.

2

2. "Now, on.

f

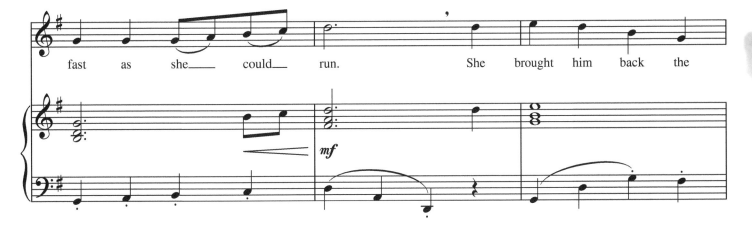

fast as she____ could____ run. She brought him back the

fin - est that was there and the sol - dier put it____ on.

f

4. "Now

sol - dier, sol - dier will you mar - ry me with your mus - ket, fife and

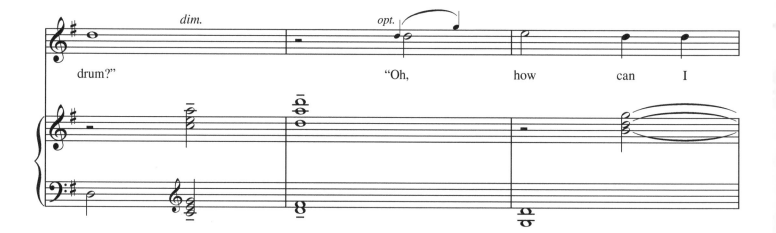

drum?" "Oh, how can I

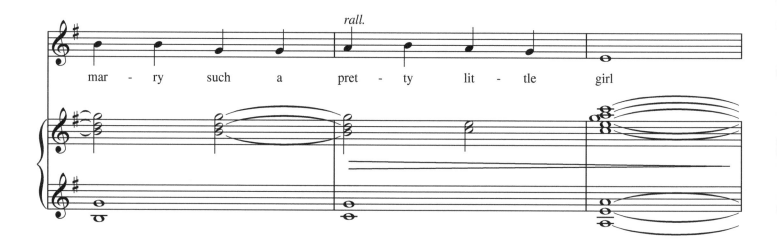

mar - ry such a pret - ty lit - tle girl

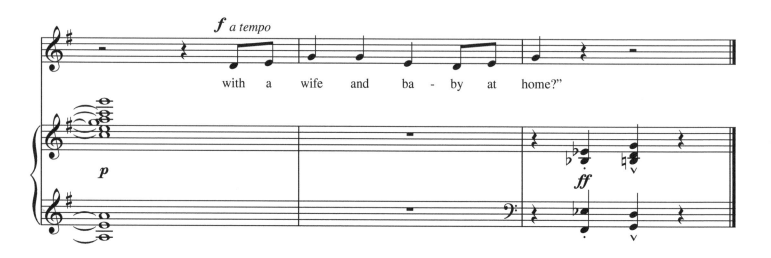

with a wife and ba - by at home?"